Original title:
Beyond the Bedtime Sky

Copyright © 2024 Creative Arts Management OÜ
All rights reserved.

Author: Cameron Blair
ISBN HARDBACK: 978-9916-90-578-4
ISBN PAPERBACK: 978-9916-90-579-1

Pastel Wonders of a Gentle Night

Soft hues paint the evening sky,
Stars blink gently, low and high.
Moonlight dances on silver streams,
Whispers cradle your tender dreams.

Sweet fragrances linger in the air,
Night's embrace is beyond compare.
Crickets serenade the stillness near,
While time stands still, suspending fear.

Across the Veil of Whispering Stars

Underneath a canvas wide and deep,
Secrets of the universe softly creep.
Echoes linger from distant worlds,
In this silence, curiosity unfurls.

Footprints trace the paths of light,
Guiding souls through the endless night.
With every twinkle, a story unfolds,
In the cosmos, where magic beholds.

Twilight's Embrace at the Edge of Sleep

Golden hues melt into gray,
Carrying dreams that gently sway.
The horizon bleeds a soft embrace,
Welcoming rest in a tranquil space.

Whispers float on a soft night breeze,
Cradled thoughts among swaying trees.
As eyelids flutter, and visions soar,
Twilight beckons, opening the door.

Wandering Feet on Astral Shores

Footprints in the stardust sand,
Wanderers drape the cosmos grand.
Galaxies hum a lullaby,
While comets blink and swiftly fly.

Waves of light crash soft and bright,
Illuminating the depths of night.
With every step upon this shore,
The universe opens, forever more.

When the Moon Sings Softly

When the moon sings softly, night takes flight,
Whispers of silver, a calming light.
Dreams wander freely, a gentle embrace,
In the quiet night, we find our place.

Stars twinkle like eyes, watching from above,
Each flicker a promise, a tale of love.
The world is at peace, cradled in dreams,
Floating on clouds, or so it seems.

Shadows dance lightly, in the moon's warm glow,
Secrets of ages in the night wind blow.
Hearts align gently, like the tides do sway,
Guided by moonlight, we drift and we play.

In the soft serenade, we lose all care,
Wrapped in the magic that fills the air.
When the moon sings softly, our spirits rise,
In this dreamy realm, we touch the skies.

Stars Unraveled in the Midnight Tapestry

In the midnight tapestry, stars intertwine,
Stories of old in a celestial line.
Each dot a vessel of light and of grace,
Weaving our dreams in a timeless space.

Galaxies whisper in shimmering tones,
Echoes of laughter, the universe's moans.
As comets rush by in a brilliant trance,
We lose ourselves in the cosmic dance.

Nebulas bloom like flowers at night,
Painting the heavens in colors so bright.
Constellations guide us through paths yet unknown,
Charting adventures in the vastness alone.

At dawn's early light, the tapestry fades,
Yet memories linger in the morning shades.
Stars unraveled gently, a night well spent,
In the heart of the cosmos, our souls are lent.

The Realm of Slumbering Wonders

In the realm of slumbering wonders we dream,
Where moonbeams shimmer and starlight gleams.
A place where time bends and moments stand still,
Each whispering breeze carries whispers that thrill.

Mountains of pillows and rivers of sleep,
The secrets of night in the shadows we keep.
Cotton candy clouds float gently above,
While echoes of laughter weave stories of love.

Colors of twilight paint visions so bright,
In the heart of the darkness, there dances light.
The wonders awaken in silence profound,
In this realm of dreams, our hopes do abound.

As dawn gently nudges us back to the day,
We carry the magic of night on our way.
In the realm of slumbering wonders so vast,
We treasure the dreams, though the night doesn't last.

Dreams Carried on a Starlit Breeze

Dreams carried on a starlit breeze,
Softly they whisper through the twilight trees.
Like petals of flowers that drift in the air,
They cradle our thoughts, tender and rare.

Moonlit reflections dance on the lake,
Mirrors of magic, a moment to take.
Each ripple a promise, each wave a caress,
In dreams carried softly, we find our finesse.

The night stretches out with an artist's hand,
Painting our visions on the soft, glowing sand.
Voices of twilight sing sweet, calm songs,
In the arms of the night, where each heart belongs.

As dawn breaks the silence, we treasure the night,
The dreams carried gently take flight in the light.
For though they may fade with the morning's embrace,
The memory lingers, a soft, warm trace.

Imagined Worlds in the Stillness of Time

In quiet corners where dreams reside,
Time whispers softly, a gentle guide.
Colors flutter like butterflies,
In a stillness where reality lies.

Moments captured in amber glow,
Lost in the depths where secrets flow.
Each heartbeat echoes through the space,
Imagination weaves a tender lace.

From shadows cast by a moonlit glance,
A tapestry woven by fate's romance.
In silence, stories unfurl their wings,
In the soft embrace that time always brings.

Here, worlds collide in the hush of night,
Each breath a spark, igniting delight.
In stillness, the cosmos begins to twine,
In imagined worlds, we find our shrine.

The Palettes of Nocturnal Wonders

Glistening stars in the velvet black,
Painted wonders on the night's track.
Moonbeams dance on the canvas wide,
Brushing dreams where shadows bide.

Whispers of night on twilight's breath,
Colors swirl in a cosmic depth.
Lavender skies mix with deep indigo,
In the silence where visions flow.

Crickets serenade the waking trees,
Their symphony floats on the evening breeze.
Each hue a story, a mystery spun,
In palettes rich where the night has run.

Underneath the celestial dome,
The heart finds peace, a place called home.
Nocturnal wonders, a fleeting glance,
In colors painted, we find our chance.

A Dance of Light and Dark

Twilight whispers a secret tune,
Where shadows gather and dreams bloom.
Light pirouettes with a gentle spark,
In a delicate dance of light and dark.

Flickers of hope in the dusk's embrace,
Each movement tells of a timeless grace.
Stars twinkle like jewels in the night,
While the world sighs under the moon's light.

They twine together in a mystical play,
As twilight fades to end of day.
In the in-between, they softly share,
A dance so intricate, beyond compare.

As dawn approaches, they gently part,
Leaving echoes in the waking heart.
A testament to their fleeting art,
This dance of light and dark shall start.

The Portal of Night's Abundant Heart

In the stillness where time does cease,
A portal opens, inviting peace.
Night's heart beats in rhythmic grace,
Welcoming souls to this sacred space.

Stars align in celestial songs,
Echoing where the mystery belongs.
Dreams cascade through the velvet veil,
In whispered tales where shadows sail.

Infinite journeys lie ahead,
Through the corridor where dreams are fed.
Each pulse of night, a tender art,
Illuminating the path to the heart.

Embrace the wonders that darkness brings,
In the essence of night, our spirit sings.
The portal glows with an endless start,
Opening wide from night's abundant heart.

A Journey through the Cosmic Veil

Stars twinkle far in the night,
Guiding ships through endless flight.
Comets blaze with fiery trails,
Charting maps of cosmic scales.

Planets dance in silent grace,
Each in its own timeless space.
Galaxies swirl, a grand ballet,
Unfolding dreams in soft array.

Nebulas bloom in pastel hues,
Painting skies with radiant views.
Time bends beneath the cosmic sigh,
A journey where spirits can fly.

The Universe's Gentle Lullaby

In the hush of velvet night,
Stars are singing, soft and bright.
Melodies of the distant past,
Echo through the heavens vast.

Whispers float on tranquil air,
Cradled in the cosmos' care.
Each note a secret of the skies,
Tales of love that never dies.

The moon casts shadows, pure and clear,
Wrapping dreams in silver cheer.
A lullaby for souls to keep,
As the universe rocks us to sleep.

Cradled in Celestial Light

Beneath the glow of stars above,
We find the warmth of endless love.
Galaxies shimmer, souls entwined,
In this vastness, solace we find.

The Milky Way, a river bright,
Carries dreams in the still night.
Light-years whisper tales untold,
Of journeys brave and hearts that bold.

In stardust pools, we float and drift,
In cosmic arms, our spirits lift.
Cradled close in the tender glow,
A dance of light, forever flow.

Whispers of the Twilight Veil

As day meets night, a hush descends,
The twilight veil, where magic blends.
Stars awaken, shy and bright,
Painting dreams across the night.

A soft breeze carries tales anew,
Of lost loves and skies so blue.
In the shadows, secrets plays,
Whispers weave through endless days.

Moonbeams drape on slumbering fields,
Nature's breath, a healing shield.
In the calm of twilight's song,
We find the place where we belong.

Stars in Our Sleepy Eyes

In the stillness of twilight's glow,
We find secrets the night would show.
Whispers dance on the gentle breeze,
As dreams unfold like fragrant tease.

Eyes that shimmer, soft and bright,
Hold the magic of starlit night.
Every twinkle, a tale unspun,
In the quiet, our hearts are won.

Drifting slowly on clouded thoughts,
We chase the dreams that time forgot.
With each blink, new worlds arise,
Lost within our sleepy eyes.

So let us wander through the night,
Chasing visions, pure and light.
Hand in hand, we'll softly glide,
Stars in our eyes, love as our guide.

The Dreamweaver's Canvas

On a canvas of velvet blue,
The Dreamweaver paints anew.
Colors swirl in mystic flight,
Crafting wonders in the night.

Every stroke a tale untold,
In shades of silver, hints of gold.
With tender care, dreams take their form,
In the heart of the quiet storm.

Each brush of fate, a path to find,
Woven threads of the wandering mind.
In this realm where wishes play,
We lose ourselves, then drift away.

So let us gaze at the stars above,
And paint our dreams with hope and love.
For on the Dreamweaver's canvas vast,
Every dream is meant to last.

Echoes of a Dreaming World

In the corners of the night,
Echoes call with soft delight.
Voices whisper like the breeze,
Carrying dreams with gentle ease.

Through the shadows, tales emerge,
Flowing forth like a quiet surge.
Every heartbeat, a melody,
In this dreamscape, wild and free.

The moonlight casts a silver hue,
Painting visions old and new.
With each sigh, we journey deep,
Into the realms of endless sleep.

So listen close, let your heart roam,
In the echoes, we find our home.
For in dreams, where hopes unfurl,
We discover a vibrant world.

Under the Soft Gaze of Night

Under the soft gaze of night,
We find solace, hearts so light.
Stars like lanterns, shine above,
Wrapping dreams in threads of love.

With every sigh, the world slows down,
As shadows dance in a silver gown.
Moments linger, sweet and rare,
In this twilight, free from care.

Time suspends in the gentle air,
While moonbeams weave a vision rare.
Hand in hand, we drift along,
The night serenades our song.

So let us cherish this embrace,
Lost together in this space.
For under the soft gaze of night,
We find our dreams take flight.

The Hidden Garden of Midnight Tales

In shadows deep, where secrets grow,
Whispers weave through night's soft glow.
Petals flutter, stories untold,
A garden blooms, with dreams of old.

Twilight dances on silver streams,
Crickets sing of faded dreams.
Beneath the stars, the heart finds peace,
In velvet nights, the troubles cease.

Forgotten paths, where silence sings,
Every step, enchantment brings.
Mossy stones, embrace the past,
In this haven, joys hold fast.

As moonlight weaves its gentle threads,
The hidden garden softly spreads.
In every corner, a new delight,
A sanctuary in the night.

Illuminations of the Inward Journey

A lantern glows within the soul,
Guiding hearts toward a common goal.
Inward paths, where shadows creep,
Awakening dreams from restless sleep.

The mind a maze, with twists and turns,
Each corner hides, a lesson learns.
With every breath, the spirit soars,
Unraveling truths behind closed doors.

Reflections dance on the still pond,
Silent echoes, a gentle bond.
Inward journey, a sacred rite,
Finding strength in the quiet light.

Illuminations softly gleam,
Leading seekers toward the dream.
In the depths, pure wisdom waits,
Unfolding tales of love and fates.

Starlit Maps to a Restful Heart

Beneath the stars, a journey starts,
Guided softly, the starlit arts.
Maps of light, drawn in the dark,
Leading the way to a tender spark.

Each point a wish, each line a dream,
In cosmic whispers, gentle streams.
Hearts find solace in night's embrace,
Tracing paths through time and space.

The moon a friend, with secrets shared,
In tranquil skies, the soul is bared.
Wanderers stroll on celestial trails,
Finding peace when hope prevails.

In this tapestry, hearts unwind,
Starlit maps are loving signs.
A restful heart, a journey bright,
Guided gently by the night.

Echoing Dreams in the Quiet Ether

In the stillness, dreams take flight,
Carried softly through the night.
Whispers linger in the air,
Echoes of wishes, light as prayer.

Time stands still, as stars align,
In quiet ether, all things combine.
Voices hum, a soothing tune,
Cradled gently by the moon.

Every heartbeat, a silent wish,
In the depths, hope's blissful swish.
Fragments dance on unseen breezes,
Mending fragments, as time pleases.

Within this calm, the spirit glows,
Echoing dreams that life bestows.
In quiet moments, truth is found,
In the ether, love's profound.

The Hush of Twilight Whispers

In twilight's calm, the shadows play,
Soft whispers float, then drift away.
The world sinks low, in shades of blue,
As night unfolds, a dream come true.

Stars awaken in the darkened sky,
Their twinkles tell of night's soft sigh.
The breeze carries a soothing song,
In this hush, we all belong.

As silence wraps the earth in peace,
Worries fade, and troubles cease.
With twilight's touch, our hearts ignite,
In stillness found, we find our light.

So let us pause and breathe it in,
In quiet moments, new dreams begin.
The hush of twilight, sweet and slow,
Invites us to where whispers flow.

Night's Lanterns Guiding the Way

Night's lanterns glow, a silver thread,
They light the path, where we are led.
Each twinkling star, a guiding spark,
  Illuminates the cool, dark park.

With every step, the shadows play,
  Dancing softly as we sway.
The moon, a keeper of our sighs,
Whispers secrets from the skies.

Paths entwined beneath the night,
  Hearts united, futures bright.
In every glow, in every beam,
We find the heart of every dream.

So follow well the stars above,
In their light, we find our love.
Night's lanterns, steady and true,
  Guide us softly, me and you.

Dreams as Light upon the Window Pane

Dreams dance lightly, like dust on glass,
A fleeting glimpse of time that pass.
They shimmer softly in the night,
As hopes take flight, a gentle light.

Each reflection tells a story new,
Of whispered wishes and skies so blue.
The window glows with dreams unspun,
A tapestry of life begun.

In shadows cast by moonlit beams,
We find ourselves within our dreams.
With every breath, a wish is made,
As night's embrace begins to fade.

So let us dream, let visions shine,
Upon the glass, our hearts align.
For in these reflections, we will find,
A world reborn, our souls entwined.

The Cadence of Night's Gentle Breath

The night unfolds, a velvet space,
With every moment, we find grace.
Stars murmur secrets in the dark,
As silence holds its gentle spark.

The moonlight weaves through tree and street,
A tender rhythm, soft and sweet.
In quietude, the heart beats slow,
With every pulse, the love we grow.

Whispers linger, like a breeze,
Caressing leaves upon the trees.
The night's embrace, a lover's sigh,
In this stillness, time drifts by.

As dreams are spun in slumber's lace,
We find ourselves in time and space.
The cadence of the night's warm breath,
A promise held, beyond all death.

The Dance of Shadows and Stars

In twilight's embrace, shadows play,
Beneath the stars, they sway and sway,
Whispers of night, a soft ballet,
As dreams unfold, and thoughts drift away.

Moonlight weaves through branches bare,
Casting spells in the cool night air,
The cosmos twirls in a sparkling glare,
While echoes of silence float everywhere.

Footsteps of night, a gentle sound,
Among the stars, lost souls are found,
In every pause, a joy profound,
As the dance of shadows spins around.

Time holds its breath, the world feels light,
In the embrace of enchanting night,
Together they twirl, in pure delight,
The shadows and stars, a wondrous sight.

A Serenade for the Sleeping Mind

In the hush of night, a lullaby flows,
With whispers of dreams, the moonlight glows,
Softly it cradles where stillness grows,
Inviting the mind to wander and doze.

Shimmering visions drift through the air,
Gentle caresses, both light and rare,
Embracing the thoughts, with tender care,
Each note a promise, a sweet affair.

Stars twinkle softly, in rhythmic refrain,
Guiding the heart through valleys of grain,
In slumber's embrace, we shed all pain,
As the serenade weaves its gentle chain.

With every sigh, the world fades away,
Nestled in dreams, where we long to stay,
The sleeping mind dances, a soft ballet,
Cradled by night, till dawn's light breaks the sway.

The Slumbering Ocean of Stars

Beneath the night's blanket, deep and vast,
A slumbering ocean, where dreams are cast,
Every star a wave, a soft contrast,
Whispering tales of the glories past.

The tides of time wash gently ashore,
With secrets hidden, and legends of lore,
Each pulse a heartbeat, forevermore,
In the ocean of stars, we endlessly explore.

Ripples of light dance on the sea,
Inviting the mind to drift and be free,
In the cosmos, we lose all decree,
Submerged in wonder, just you and me.

Awash in the glow of celestial gleam,
We float on the thoughts of a tender dream,
In the slumbering ocean, we gently beam,
Floating on clouds, like a vivid theme.

Cosmic Threads of Sleep's Weave

In the cradle of night, the stars align,
Weaving cosmic threads, so soft and fine,
Embracing our slumber like aged wine,
Entwining our thoughts in a languid line.

Each twinkle a stitch in the tapestry bright,
Sewing together the fabric of night,
With every breath, we ascend to flight,
As dreams intertwine with the celestial light.

The universe hums a gentle refrain,
Carrying whispers of joy and pain,
In the web of slumber where we remain,
Bound by the magic that speaks our name.

When morning beckons with its golden hue,
We rise with the dawn, refreshed and new,
Yet in heart and mind, the stars still strew,
Cosmic threads that connect me and you.

The Carriers of Midnight's Secrets

In shadows deep, the whispers play,
Through twilight's veil, they gently sway.
Secrets held in silvered beams,
Carried forth on moonlit dreams.

A tapestry of stars unspools,
Beneath the gaze of ancient fools.
They dance in silence, shadows blend,
In midnight's arms, the secrets mend.

The night unfurls its hidden art,
Each flicker lights a heavy heart.
In every twinkle, stories bind,
Inscribed in dark, yet brightly signed.

So listen close, as night bequeaths,
The tales entwined in starlit wreaths.
For carriers of secrets lie,
In every breath beneath the sky.

The Alchemy of Night's Embrace

In velvet dusk, the world's reborn,
Where whispers swirl, and dreams are worn.
Night's embrace, a tender touch,
Transforms the mundane into such.

With starlit threads, the darkness weaves,
A potion brewed from heart's believes.
Alchemy of cosmic lore,
Unlocks the dreams that life ignores.

The moonlit path, a sacred course,
Guides the wanderers with gentle force.
In every shadow, light will chase,
The magic found in night's embrace.

So breathe in deep the night's sweet air,
Let stardust sprinkle everywhere.
For within the dark, the light shall rise,
In love awakened beneath the skies.

A Serenade for the Starry-eyed

Oh wanderer of the cosmic seas,
With dreams as vast as galaxies.
A serenade for hearts that long,
To find their place where stars belong.

In midnight's hue, your spirit flies,
A melody that brightly ties.
To every twinkle, hope is sown,
In symphonies of night you've grown.

Each star a note, each glance a song,
In harmony where you belong.
With every breath, let stardust flow,
Embrace the magic, let it grow.

So take your dreams, let them ignite,
In realms where day is kissed by night.
For in your heart, the universe cries,
A serenade for the starry-eyed.

Keys to the Cosmic Dreamland

In realms where shadows softly gleam,
The cosmic keys unlock the dream.
With every step, the stars align,
To guide the heart through space and time.

A sparkling path where wishes flow,
In whispered tones, the starlights glow.
Each key a portal to the vast,
Where future melds with phantom past.

The moonlight casts its silver spell,
In secret realms where heartbeats swell.
Unlock the doors of endless skies,
And let your spirit freely rise.

So gather dreams, your essence blend,
In cosmic fields that never end.
With every key, a journey grand,
To find your place in dreamland's span.

A Journey through the Nebula of Night

In the silence of twilight's glow,
Stars emerge, putting on a show.
Whispers of dreams softly unfold,
Mapping the skies, a tale untold.

Winding paths of cosmic grace,
A dance of shadows, a vast embrace.
Galaxies swirl, a celestial sea,
Leading our hearts, wild and free.

Each twinkle a piece of ancient lore,
Guiding the wanderers to explore.
In the expanse where wishes ignite,
We journey forth through the nebula of night.

Starlit Stories for the Adventurous Soul

Close your eyes, let dreams take flight,
Beneath the veil of the starry night.
With every twinkle, tales unfold,
Adventures await in the cosmic cold.

Where comets race and echoes sing,
A universe ripe with wondrous things.
Each star a beacon, bright and bold,
Writing stories worth more than gold.

Into the depths, where magic flows,
An adventurous spirit forever grows.
In the tapestry woven by starlight,
Our souls ignite in the endless night.

The Enchantment of the Darkest Hour

When shadows deepen, and daylight fades,
Mysteries linger in twilight's shades.
The moon rises high, casting her glow,
Enchanting the world with secrets to know.

Silence blankets the sleeping earth,
In the darkest hour, lies hidden worth.
Dreamers awaken to visions unchained,
In splendor of night, our spirits remained.

Stars like lanterns lead us through,
Every heartbeat a magic imbue.
Whispers of night dance through the air,
In the enchantment, we find our care.

Celestial Adventures in Dreamland

In dreamland's realm, the stars align,
A tapestry spun, nearly divine.
Planets beckon with a twinkling call,
Inviting us deeper, into their thrall.

Floating on clouds of shimmering light,
We travel through realms, oh, what a sight!
Each moment alive with wonder and glee,
In celestial adventures, we wander free.

Comets streak past with fiery trails,
Carrying wishes on gentle gales.
With hearts intertwined, we embrace the dream,
In cosmic dances, we flow like a stream.

Comets and Cottons of Slumber

In the hush of twilight's glow,
Cottons cradle dreams to sow.
Comets dance across the sky,
Whispering secrets, flying high.

Children nestled, soft in bed,
Stars alight above their head.
Fleeting visions drift and gleam,
Carried softly on a dream.

Moonlight weaves a gentle thread,
Stitching stories in their head.
Comets blaze, a fleeting spark,
Guiding souls through night's dark park.

With each sigh, the world turns slow,
In slumber's arms, all hearts will glow.
Comets fade, yet dreams remain,
In the quiet, love's refrain.

Nocturnal Tales of Wonder

Underneath the silver moon,
Whispers float, a haunting tune.
Tales of wonder softly spun,
In the dark, adventures run.

Owls are calling, secrets shared,
Through the forest, dreams are bared.
Magic lingers in the air,
Floating softly without a care.

Stars are ink on velvet skies,
Telling stories, ancient ties.
Every shimmer, every light,
Holds a chapter of the night.

Slumbering hearts in shadows deep,
Swaying gently, lulled by sleep.
Nocturnal tales forever spun,
Await the dawn when dreams are done.

The Ethereal Dance of Nighttime

In shadows deep, the night awakes,
An ethereal dance that softly breaks.
Winds entwine with velvet skies,
As the world beneath it lies.

Stars pirouette in a cosmic ball,
Echoes of light, a siren's call.
Moonbeams glide on silken streams,
Whispering softly through our dreams.

Night unfolds with a gentle sigh,
Painting art through the still sky.
Every twinkle, every blaze,
Guides our hearts in night's warm haze.

Dancing with shadows, we lose our way,
In the embrace of night's soft sway.
The ethereal dance, a sacred rite,
Revealing magic hidden from sight.

Visions from the Silken Sky

Drifting softly through the night,
Visions flicker, bold and bright.
Clouds like silk, a gentle fold,
Cradle secrets yet untold.

In the stillness, dreams take flight,
Against the backdrop of the night.
Stars are stories, constellations weave,
In each twinkle, we believe.

Moonlit paths of silver beams,
Guide our hearts through whispered dreams.
Every shimmer, every sigh,
Takes us higher, toward the sky.

Visions linger, soft and sweet,
As the night and day compete.
Silken threads of light draw near,
In the darkness, love is clear.

The Voyage to Dreamscape Haven

Set sail on whispers soft,
Where lullabies gently drift.
The stars above twinkle bright,
In the night, our spirits lift.

Waves of silver, calm and still,
Carry us to realms unknown.
Guided by the moon's sweet glow,
In this space, we'll roam alone.

Clouds like pillows, dreams entwined,
Each moment feels like a sigh.
As we navigate the breeze,
Hope and wonder draw us high.

Together, hand in hand we glide,
Beyond the shores of earthly pain.
To Dreamscape Haven, we will go,
In the night, we shall remain.

When the Moonlight Paints the Sky

Softly shines the silver light,
Casting shadows on the ground.
Stars awake from restful night,
In their sparkle, dreams abound.

Gentle breezes, whispers low,
Carry secrets of the night.
In their dance, we come to know,
Everything will soon be right.

Clouds like lace drift overhead,
As we wander hand in hand.
In this moment, fears all shed,
Together, we will understand.

When the moonlight paints the sky,
We will find our hearts align.
In quiet magic, we will fly,
Through night's curtain, dreams entwine.

Celestial Sojourn at Dusk's Horizon

Twilight beckons, colors blend,
As day gives in to night's embrace.
Stars awaken, journeys send,
To the heavens, we make haste.

Crickets sing a lullaby,
While the air grows cool and still.
At dusk's horizon, we shall fly,
On the wings of dreams, we thrill.

Veils of twilight gently fall,
Painting worlds with vibrant hues.
In this peace, we hear the call,
Of the cosmos, vast and new.

Celestial paths we'll explore,
With each star, a story told.
In this sojourn, we'll adore,
The wonders of the night unfold.

Journeys Through the Starry Abyss

In the depth of void we sail,
Where silent echoes softly hum.
Stars like candles gently pale,
In this vast and wondrous dome.

Nebulas weave a tapestry,
Colors swirl in cosmic dance.
In the dark, we're wild and free,
Lost in fate's endless romance.

Galaxies spin, time stands still,
Each moment holds an endless grace.
With every turn, our dreams fulfill,
As we drift through this endless space.

Together we shall wander far,
In the starry abyss we dive.
The universe is our memoir,
In these journeys, we will thrive.

A Waltz Amongst the Nebulae

In the hush of night, stars gleam,
Whispers dance in stellar streams.
Colors swirl, a cosmic grace,
In velvet skies, they find their place.

Twinkling lights in gentle flight,
We sway beneath the cloak of night.
Galaxies twirl, a soft embrace,
Lost in dreams, time leaves no trace.

Nebulae weave their glowing thread,
Stories told of worlds long fled.
Floating through this vast ballet,
We waltz where shadows softly play.

Hold my hand in this twilight glow,
Where the secrets of the cosmos flow.
In the depths of space, we reside,
As stardust whispers, we confide.

Enchanted Moments in Cosmic Twilight

A shimmer glows on the horizon's line,
Time stands still, a dream divine.
Moments linger, soft and rare,
As the universe breathes in air.

Nebulas wrap in colors bright,
Cradling whispers of ancient light.
Each second pulses with delight,
In this enchanted cosmic night.

The stars align in a perfect dance,
Inviting us into a trance.
With every blink, a new embrace,
In this eternal, sacred space.

Threads of fate begin to weave,
In secrets only stars believe.
Moments cherished, hearts held tight,
In twilight's glow, love takes flight.

Navigating the Astral Seas

Across the waves of dark expanse,
We sail on currents, a cosmic dance.
Stars our beacons, guiding light,
Navigating through the endless night.

Planets rise and fall like tides,
In the galaxy, our journey abides.
With constellations as our chart,
We set our course, two souls, one heart.

Galaxies swirl, a vast embrace,
In this voyage, we find our place.
Comets streak with tales untold,
As we drift deeper into the cold.

Each moment crafted in starlit hues,
In the astral seas, we chase our muse.
Together we roam, wild and free,
Forever sailing this mystery.

The Enigma of Quiet Cosmos

In the silence of the cosmic weave,
A riddle whispered, hearts believe.
Stars blink softly, hidden clues,
In the night, their secrets fuse.

Questions linger in the dark,
Each twinkle, just a fleeting spark.
Galaxies spin, a hush profound,
In this enigma, peace is found.

Time drips slowly, like a stream,
Amongst the stars, we softly dream.
Each breath we take blends with space,
In the quiet of this boundless place.

What lies beyond the cosmic veil?
In silent wonders, we set our sail.
Together we search the endless sky,
In the stillness, we learn to fly.

Voyage Amongst the Flickering Stars

In the night sky, ships of light,
Sailing softly, hearts take flight.
Guided by the twinkling grace,
We drift through dreams in endless space.

Galaxies whisper secrets deep,
Stories sung by stars that keep.
Waves of wonder, vast and wide,
Our voyage sails where hopes abide.

Each comet trails a blazing tail,
Adventures born on stardust trails.
With every pulse, the universe sings,
As we dance through all its offerings.

Beneath this dome of glowing night,
We find our way in pure delight.
Voyagers bound by cosmic thread,
In the flickering stars, dreams are fed.

The Forgotten Stories Amidst the Shadows

Whispers linger in the dark,
Forgotten tales leave their mark.
Shadows dance on ancient walls,
Echoes of past, their silent calls.

Beneath the moon's soft, pale glow,
Lost memories begin to flow.
Stories written in twilight's hue,
Awaiting hearts that seek the true.

Every corner holds a spark,
Every whisper, every lark.
In the quiet, the past unspools,
Revealing truths in shadowed schools.

Forgotten stories softly thread,
Weaving through the words unsaid.
In the silence, listen close,
To the tales that time can boast.

The Garden Where Dreams Flower

Among the blooms, wishes unfold,
Colorful petals, dreams untold.
In every garden, hope takes root,
Nurtured by love, sweet and astute.

Sunlight streaming through the leaves,
A tapestry that our heart weaves.
Butterflies dance, a ballet rare,
In this haven, pure and fair.

Raindrops nourish, silver and bright,
Dreams blossom gently, taking flight.
With every fragrance, a soft sigh,
In this paradise, spirits rise high.

Time flows like a gentle stream,
In the garden where we dream.
Nestled amongst petals' embrace,
We find our peace in this sacred space.

Tales of the Unseen Moonbeams

In the dark, where shadows hide,
Unseen moonbeams softly glide.
Whispers of light, they weave their thread,
Tales untold, where dreams are fed.

With every glimmer, a story spins,
Of unseen worlds and secret sins.
Through twilight's veil, they softly play,
Guiding lost souls along their way.

Mysteries dance in the silver glow,
Unveiling truths that few may know.
In the silence, we hear their call,
Tales of wonder, embracing all.

Let us listen, hearts open wide,
To the moonbeams that softly bide.
For within their light, we shall find,
The stories that bless both heart and mind.

Reflections in the Midnight Mirror

In shadows deep, secrets swirl,
A silent gaze, a hidden world.
Whispers echo, time stands still,
The midnight mirror, dreams fulfill.

Flickering lights from unknown shores,
Fragments of hope behind closed doors.
Each reflection tells a story,
In this twilight, seek the glory.

Faces drift like autumn leaves,
Caught in webs that memory weaves.
Moments captured, fleeting sight,
In the mirror of the night.

Dancing flames of thoughts unchained,
Reveal the fears that once remained.
As dawn approaches, shadows yield,
To the visions the night revealed.

Moonlit Pathways to the Unknown

Beneath the stars, a trail unfolds,
Where dreams reside and fate beholds.
Moonlight guides with gentle trust,
Leading hearts through night's soft rust.

Every step, a new embrace,
Whispers linger, time and space.
In the silence, secrets hum,
As shadows stretch, the night becomes.

To wander far, to seek and find,
The hidden truth that haunts the mind.
With courage, take the way unplanned,
For magic blooms where dreams will stand.

A journey bright, with shadows near,
Each heartbeat sings, dispelling fear.
Moonlit pathways, vast and wide,
Call to wanderers who bide.

Constellations of a Sleepy Heart

Stars align in velvet skies,
Whispers of love in lullabies.
With every twinkle, dreams take flight,
In the cosmos, hearts unite.

Nights of wonder, stories weave,
In the hush, restless souls believe.
Constellations dance above,
Guiding all to find their love.

The sleepy heart begins to soar,
In the calm, it seeks for more.
Galaxies of feelings spark,
Illuminate the silent dark.

In this canvas, vast and grand,
Feelings rise like grains of sand.
Sleepy hearts, in dreams conferred,
Find their voice in starlit words.

Tales Told by Firefly Sparks

In the dusky, fading light,
Fireflies blink with tales so bright.
Each little flicker, a story told,
Of summer nights and hearts of gold.

They weave through trees with magic grace,
Lighting paths in a hidden space.
With laughter echoing in the air,
Whispers linger, dreams laid bare.

Adventures found in shadows near,
Echoes of joy, sweet and clear.
Sparks of memory, dancing light,
Carry the heart through the night.

As darkness deepens, tales ignite,
The firefly sparks in flight delight.
In each glow, a life to share,
Weaving dreams beyond compare.

Nightfall's Enchanted Realm

Whispers of shadows gently glide,
Stars awaken, casting dreams wide.
Moonlight dances on velvet night,
Embracing the world in silver light.

Every tree holds secrets deep,
Beneath their boughs, the spirits creep.
Crickets sing in harmonious tune,
As fireflies twinkle beneath the moon.

Mysteries roam the starlit glade,
In this realm where time seems to fade.
A breeze carries tales of old,
Of wishes made and dreams foretold.

In the heart of night, magic swells,
Where silence speaks and darkness dwells.
Close your eyes and drift afar,
To Nightfall's realm, beneath a star.

The Gravity of a Midnight Wish

In the quiet of the midnight hour,
Dreams awaken, bloom like a flower.
A wish releases into the night,
Caught on the edge of sheer delight.

Branches sway with a secret grace,
Time slows in this enchanted space.
Stars align, destiny's kiss,
The gravity of a midnight wish.

With each heartbeat, hope takes flight,
Journeying through the endless night.
Embers flicker in the dark,
Igniting desires, creating spark.

Hold on tight to whispered dreams,
For in the stillness, nothing seems.
The night bears witness to our quest,
As midnight wishes find their rest.

Lullabies in the Cosmic Sea

Cradled by stars, in the cosmic sea,
The universe sings soft melodies.
Galaxies swirl in a tender embrace,
While dreams drift on in infinite space.

Nebulas wrap in pastel light,
Painting wonders that dance in the night.
Each lullaby whispers tender and sweet,
Carrying hearts on stardust's fleet.

Sailing through skies where comets fly,
Underneath the vast, endless sky.
The cosmos hums with ethereal grace,
Lulling us softly, in time and place.

With every twinkle, a story unfolds,
In the cosmic sea where magic beholds,
A lullaby plays, soothing our fears,
Cradled in dreams through the endless years.

Floating on the Cloud's Silken Thread

Suspended high in a world divine,
On clouds woven with dreams that shine.
Drifting softly, weightlessly free,
Floating onward, lost in reverie.

The sun dips low, casting a glow,
Painting horizons in hues that flow.
Each moment a treasure, each breath a gift,
As spirits awaken and hearts uplift.

Whispers of wind guide each glide,
Carrying wishes on the morning tide.
With feathered dreams and laughter's sound,
On soft silken threads, we are unbound.

In the embrace of a sky so wide,
We dance on air with joy and pride.
Floating, we find our hearts converge,
On the cloud's silken thread, we emerge.

Floating on Starlight's Whisper

In twilight's glow, we drift and sway,
Among the stars where night meets day.
A gentle breeze, a soft caress,
Wrapped in dreams, we find our rest.

Whispers echo through the trees,
Carried forth on tranquil seas.
Each twinkling light, a voice so clear,
Calling us to linger near.

With every sigh, the shadows dance,
In starlit realms, we take our chance.
To weave our hopes, to let them soar,
Forever grounded, yet wanting more.

So let us float, no need to fear,
For starlight's warmth draws us near.
In the silence, dreams take flight,
Floating softly on starlight's light.

The Solace of Distant Suns

In the night, the whispers call,
From distant suns, a gentle thrall.
Their warm embrace, a soothing balm,
In darkness deep, they keep us calm.

The universe sings a lullaby,
To carry hopes on wings that fly.
Each spark of light tells tales untold,
Of ancient dreams and wishes bold.

As we gaze into the vast unknown,
We find the paths our hearts have sown.
A cosmic dance of fate and chance,
In every twinkle, there's romance.

Beneath the glow of radiant skies,
The solace found in starry ties.
Holding tight, our spirits run,
Forever drawn to distant suns.

Chasing Dreams on Moonlit Breezes

Through silver rays, our laughter flows,
We chase the dreams that moonlight throws.
With every step, the night unfolds,
In darkened skies, our fate beholds.

Adrift on waves of quiet night,
We dance beneath the soft, pale light.
Whispers of hope, like petals fall,
Guiding us through the shadow's thrall.

With every breeze, our spirits soar,
Embracing dreams we can't ignore.
Each heartbeat echoes in the air,
A melody of love and care.

As morning's glow begins to creep,
We hold our dreams, forever keep.
Chasing whispers on moonlit streams,
In the night, we live our dreams.

Starlight Strands of Sleepy Thoughts

In the quiet of night, we pause and breathe,
As starlight strands weave dreams beneath.
A tapestry of thoughts, so rare,
Cloth of wonder, woven with care.

Sleepy eyes gaze at the cosmic dance,
While hearts entwine in a sweet romance.
Landing softly on the shores of night,
Where every shadow seems to ignite.

With gentle sighs, our wishes bloom,
In fleeting moments, we dance in gloom.
Starlight blankets our restless mind,
In its embrace, true peace we find.

So close your eyes and drift away,
On starlit paths where dreams can play.
With strands of light, your thoughts will guide,
In sleepy realms, let love abide.

The Moon's Gentle Embrace

In the stillness of the night,
Silver beams dance with delight.
Whispers soft on the breeze,
Nature sighs, the heart at ease.

Bathed in light, shadows play,
Stars above guide the way.
Dreams unfold with each glance,
In the moonlight, souls enhance.

Night's cool kiss upon the skin,
A secret world waits within.
Every glow tells a tale,
As we drift on night's pale sail.

Held in arms of softest light,
Cradled in the endless night.
The Moon's love, a gentle chase,
A soothing tune, a warm embrace.

Dancing with Night's Veil

Beneath the velvet sky so bright,
Stars shimmer with pure delight.
Night's breath whispers through the trees,
A waltz that's carried by the breeze.

In shadows deep, spirits swirl,
Weaving dreams in a dusky whirl.
Moonbeams twirl in a graceful dance,
Enticing hearts with each glance.

Mysteries in the night unfold,
As the stories of starlight are told.
Time stands still, a moment rare,
In this embrace, nothing can compare.

With laughter soft, we take our chance,
Lost in wonder, caught in a trance.
Dancing free with night's veil near,
Our souls entwined, the path is clear.

Secrets of the Twilight Canvas

Brushstrokes of dusk paint the skies,
A canvas of dreams and silent sighs.
Colors blend as daylight fades,
In twilight's grace, beauty invades.

Softly the stars begin to gleam,
A tapestry woven with every dream.
Hues of purple, gold, and gray,
Secrets linger, hidden away.

In this hour of whispered lore,
Magic reigns and spirits soar.
Nature's breath, a gentle muse,
With twilight's spell, we cannot lose.

Each moment feels like a sweet embrace,
In the twilight's warm, tender space.
A world alive with stories told,
In secrets kept, we find our gold.

Midnight's Hidden Symphony

In the heart of night, silence sings,
A symphony of subtle things.
Soft notes of moonlight gently swell,
As shadows weave their mystic spell.

Stars hum sweetly, a cosmic tune,
While dreams awaken beneath the moon.
Every whisper, a note in flight,
Crafting magic in the night.

The wind carries tales ancient and deep,
As nature joins in a dance to keep.
In midnight's arms, we lose our way,
To the rhythm of night's ballet.

Tune into the world, so finely spun,
As the symphony plays, we all become one.
Midnight's music, a secret balm,
Holding us close, entwined and calm.

The Lantern of Dreams

In the twilight, shadows wane,
A flicker bright, call it by name.
Guiding whispers through the haze,
    Illuminate the winding maze.

Softly glows the silver light,
Cradling wishes, holding tight.
Each soft glance, a fleeting spark,
Leading hearts through realms so dark.

Through the night, our hopes will soar,
On wings of dreams, forevermore.
Embrace the magic, let it stream,
In the warmth of the lantern's beam.

Awake, asleep, we weave our fate,
The lantern waits, it won't be late.
With every heartbeat, fears release,
    In the glow, we find our peace.

A Tapestry of Night's Soft Embrace

Stars align in velvet skies,
A quilt of dreams where midnight lies.
Threads of silver, whispers low,
Weaving tales of love's sweet flow.

Each twinkling gem, a wish unspun,
In the calm, where hearts have won.
Bathed in shadows, softly glide,
Where secrets of the night reside.

Crickets serenade the moon,
Nature's lullaby, a gentle tune.
Wrapped in magic, softly near,
The night's embrace, forever dear.

Tapestry of life unfolds,
In silver strands, our dreams retold.
By the dawn, we'll rise anew,
Together bound, me and you.

Secrets of the Pillow Fort Kingdom

In a fortress made of dreams,
Pillow towers and sunlight beams.
Whispers shared in velvet rooms,
A kingdom born where magic blooms.

Cushions, soft as clouds above,
Holding secrets wrapped in love.
Every giggle echoes clear,
In our fort, there's naught to fear.

Adventures call from every seam,
A place to chase a fleeting dream.
Beneath the blankets, worlds unfurl,
In our heart's delight, we twirl.

As we laugh, the night draws near,
In this realm, the stars appear.
Together here, we'll find our light,
In the fort, we claim the night.

The Infinite Canvas of Restful Night

Stars are brushed on midnight's page,
An artist's fingers set the stage.
Each twinkle, a story spun,
On this canvas, dreams begun.

Moonlight paints in silver hues,
Softly waking slumbered views.
Whispers of the dreams we share,
In the peace, there's love's sweet air.

Infinite skies, our canvas wide,
Coloring nights where hopes abide.
With every breath, our spirits rise,
Creating art in cosmic skies.

As the dawn begins to break,
Every moment, hearts will wake.
A new creation waits in sight,
On the canvas of the night.

Stars that Dance on Dream's Doorstep

In the twilight's gentle glow,
Stars awaken, ready to flow.
They twirl and spin in cosmic grace,
As dreams unfold in endless space.

Soft whispers thread through the night,
Guiding hearts with silver light.
Each flicker tells a tale untold,
Of wishes cast and hopes of old.

Beneath the vast and starlit dome,
The universe sings, calling us home.
In their dance, we find our place,
A fleeting moment, a warm embrace.

So let us dream, let visions soar,
With stars that dance forevermore.
On dream's doorstep, we shall stay,
While magic weaves through night and day.

Echoes of Night's Gentle Lullaby

In the stillness of the night,
Soft lullabies take flight.
Whispers weave through the air,
Cradling souls with tender care.

A symphony of stars above,
Sings the secrets of our love.
Each note a promise, sweet and clear,
In echoes that only hearts can hear.

Moonlight dances on the ground,
As dreams in silence swirl around.
The universe hums, a soothing sound,
In the harmony that we have found.

With every heartbeat, night draws near,
Wrapping us in dreams sincere.
Echoes of love in every sigh,
As we soar beneath the sky.

The Dreamcatcher's Embrace

In the woven webs of night,
Dreams are caught in gentle light.
The dreamcatcher spins and twirls,
Guarding hopes of boys and girls.

With each thread, a story spun,
Whispered wishes, one by one.
As shadows dance and visions play,
In its embrace, fears drift away.

The stars above, like jewels bright,
Illuminate the path of night.
In dreams, we find our way to soar,
Past the realms, to distant shores.

The dreamcatcher stands so strong,
Holding the magic all night long.
In its arms, we find our peace,
A sanctuary where dreams never cease.

Secrets Hidden in Celestial Hues

In the canvas of the night,
Celestial hues take flight.
Secrets twinkle in the dark,
Painting skies with every spark.

Whispers of the universe call,
Reminding us we're part of it all.
Each star a story, each planet a rhyme,
Guarding wonders through space and time.

Among the nebulae's embrace,
Lies the essence of our grace.
In every shade, a tale to tell,
Of love, of heart, of hope that dwells.

So look above, let your spirit rise,
In secrets hidden beneath the skies.
The cosmos holds what we seek true,
In celestial hues, our spirits renew.

Whispers of the Midnight Vale

In shadows deep where soft winds sigh,
The willows weep, the owls will cry.
Stars shimmer bright, a silver trail,
Secrets shared in the midnight vale.

Echoes dance on a silent breeze,
Moonlight spills through the ancient trees.
Gentle whispers in the dark,
Nature's hymn, a tender spark.

Footsteps linger on the dew-kissed grass,
Moments fleeting, as shadows pass.
With every sigh, the heart can feel,
The magic found in the midnight vale.

Time suspends, as if to hold,
Dreams awakened, stories told.
In this realm, where spirits sail,
We find our peace in the midnight vale.

Celestial Dreams Awaken

Underneath the starlit sky,
Wishes soar, like birds on high.
Nebulas swirl in twilight's glow,
Celestial dreams begin to flow.

Galaxies twinkle, a cosmic sea,
Lifting hearts, allowing to be.
Each dream a spark, ignited bright,
Awakened souls dance in the night.

Whispers of hope in twilight's breath,
Promises made, no hint of death.
We close our eyes, let time be still,
As dreams unfold with gentle will.

Through ethereal paths, we wander free,
In the cosmos, our spirits see.
Celestial wonders touch and break,
In the silence, our hearts awake.

In the Quiet of Starlit Hours

In the calm of the night, stars gleam,
Softly shining, like whispers of dream.
The world slows down, shadows play,
In starlit hours, we drift away.

Crickets sing their nightly tune,
The silver crescent cradles the moon.
With every breath, the stillness calls,
In this peace, our spirit enthralls.

Time flows gently, like a sigh,
Beneath the blanket of the sky.
In quietude, we seek and find,
The solace in the starlit mind.

Moments linger, serene and sweet,
In the embrace where hearts can meet.
Lost in whispers, twilight's power,
In the quiet of starlit hours.

Lullabies of the Astral Realm

Dreams drift on a cosmic wave,
Where stardust swirls, the heart we crave.
In the still, a soft voice hums,
Lullabies as the starlight comes.

The universe wraps in gentle folds,
Stories of ages quietly told.
In the night, a sweet embrace,
Astral lullabies find their place.

Floating softly on celestial streams,
Awakening hearts igniting dreams.
With every note, the world feels whole,
In harmony, we touch the soul.

As comets pass and starlight glows,
In the silence, a calmness flows.
Within this song, forever dwell,
Lullabies of the astral realm.

Serene Journeys through Darkened Skies

Beneath a sky of midnight hue,
Whispers of stars dance and twine.
Gentle breezes call me through,
To discover realms where dreams align.

Softly gliding on twilight's breath,
I trace the paths where shadows play.
Each moment blooms as I forget,
The weight of worlds that fade away.

In silent realms where silence sings,
I drift on currents made of light.
Embracing all that time now brings,
Through darkened skies, my heart takes flight.

A tapestry of night unfolds,
With secrets woven in its seams.
In journeys made of starlit gold,
I find my way within my dreams.

The Velvet Pathway to Dreamland

A pathway draped in velvet night,
Where wishes weave like silver threads.
Each step embraces pure delight,
Adventuring where hope still treads.

Among the stars, in shadows deep,
I wander soft through calming mists.
With every turn, the world I keep,
A treasure chest of untold gifts.

The moonlight spills its gentle glow,
As dreams awaken from their rest.
In whispered tales, the dreamers know,
Their hearts entwined, forever blessed.

Thus I traverse this hallowed ground,
In search of peace where spirits soar.
Upon this path, sweet love is found,
In dreamland's arms forevermore.

Soaring Through the Galactic Slumber

Through cosmic fields where starlight sleeps,
I soar on wings of endless grace.
In silent dreams where the universe keeps,
I find my place in timeless space.

Galaxies whisper soft arrhythms,
As comets trail my fleeting dreams.
In this vast realm of vibrant prisms,
I dance in harmony, or so it seems.

With every breath, I chase the dawn,
Among the hues of twilight's glow.
Soaring high, never withdrawn,
In galactic slumber, I gently flow.

As stars align to greet my flight,
I etch my dreams in celestial sands.
Among the whispers of the night,
I journey forth through cosmic lands.

Shadows of the Celestial Tides

In twilight's kiss where shadows blend,
The ocean sings with stars alight.
Each wave a story, every bend,
Reflects the dance of day and night.

Celestial tides embrace the shore,
Unraveling secrets of the sea.
In gentle rhythms, hear the lore,
Of worlds beyond, waiting for me.

The moon descends with silver grace,
While whispers curl in salt-filled air.
In shadowed depths, I find my place,
As tides of wonder draw me near.

Through whispers soft and twilight's sigh,
I weave the magic of the stars.
In shadows deep, I learn to fly,
Embracing love that knows no bars.

The Radiance of Sleepy Skies

The dusk unfolds with gentle grace,
Where whispers dance through twilight's lace,
Stars begin their quiet show,
In the arms of night, we softly glow.

Dreams take flight on wings of light,
Casting shadows, glimmers bright,
Each sigh a tale, each hush a sigh,
Beneath the canvas of the sky.

Moonbeams weave through nighttime's thread,
Bathing the world in dreams widespread,
As time slows down, we find our peace,
In the stillness, worries cease.

Awake within this cosmic sea,
Where souls drift in harmony,
The radiance of sleepy skies,
Lulls the heart and opens eyes.

Beneath the Canopy of Wishful Thinking

In the forest of the imagination,
Where hope grows with every sensation,
Leaves of dreams whisper and sway,
Guiding lost hearts along the way.

Branches stretch with tales untold,
Laden with wishes, bright and bold,
A sanctuary for the heart's delight,
Beneath the canopy, veiled in light.

Soft shadows play on the forest floor,
Echoing laughter from days of yore,
Each step forward rings of chance,
In this refuge, we find our dance.

With every thought, the world expands,
Infinite realms within our hands,
Beneath the boughs, we take to flight,
In the realm of wishful night.

Floating on Dreams like Autumn Leaves

Golden hues embrace the air,
Whispers of change, soft and rare,
Leaves release, drifting with ease,
Floating on dreams like autumn leaves.

Beneath the trees, the world is still,
Time slows down with each gentle thrill,
In this moment, we find reprieve,
In the calm, our hearts believe.

As colors shift, the past retreats,
Carried by winds, each memory greets,
The symphony of change deceives,
Floating on dreams like autumn leaves.

In the rustle, stories unfold,
Of love and laughter, dreams retold,
We dance in the warmth of golden eves,
Finding solace in these woven leaves.

The Symphony of Night's Serendipity

Under the veil of a starlit sky,
Echoes hum as the night drifts by,
A serenade of whispered sighs,
The symphony of fate aligns.

Moonlight filters through the trees,
Dancing shadows whisper with ease,
Each note a promise, a gentle plea,
In the stillness, we are free.

Melodies of dreams intertwine,
With heartbeats beating, soft and fine,
As time stands still and moments freeze,
In the rhythm of night's sweet breeze.

Where serendipity blooms and glows,
In every heartbeat, magic flows,
The night reveals its tender art,
In this symphony, we find our heart.

Celestial Reflections in the Midnight Seine

Beneath the twinkling stars, they glide,
Ripples shimmer like silver thread.
Whispers of lovers softly confide,
In moonlit waters, dreams are fed.

The Seine reflects a world so bright,
Each wave a canvas, tales arise.
Night's embrace, a soft delight,
Heartfelt secrets beneath the skies.

Echoes of laughter, shadows dance,
A gentle breeze, a sweet refrain.
In this moment, lost in trance,
Eternal love flows through the vein.

Stars align in cosmic grace,
As time suspends, we drift away.
In midnight's arms, we find our place,
Celestial dreams guide our stay.

Letters Written in the Starlit Ether

Across the night, a pen does glide,
Words crafted with a lover's heart.
In starlit ether, hopes reside,
A whispered promise, never depart.

Ink flows like rivers, soft and true,
Each letter formed with tender care.
Secrets wrapped in a sky so blue,
Each thought a wish, a silent prayer.

The moon eavesdrops, a loyal friend,
Holding stories of our delight.
In every line, a message send,
Written softly in the night.

As dawn approaches, ink may fade,
But memories linger like the sun.
In every heartbeat, love conveyed,
In starlit ether, we are one.

The Aether Where Dreams Take Flight

In whispered realms where shadows play,
The aether calls to wandering souls.
With every breath, they drift away,
Chasing dreams as the night unfolds.

On silken clouds, where wishes soar,
Hope floats gently on the breeze.
Each heartbeat yearns for something more,
In this realm, our spirits ease.

Stars illuminate the path ahead,
Guiding us through the darkened skies.
In every dream, a thread is led,
Unraveling truths and sweet goodbyes.

The dawn will break, yet we shall stay,
In aether's arms, we'll find our way.
To dance with hope through endless night,
In shimmering worlds, we take our flight.

Enigmas in the Silent Night

In velvet shadows, mysteries dwell,
Whispers of secrets, softly spoken.
The moon guards tales she knows so well,
In silent night, no vow is broken.

Stars above twinkle with intent,
Like eyes observing all we dream.
Each heart a riddle, gently bent,
Unraveling life's elusive theme.

Through the dusk, echoes of the past,
Dance with the present, entwine the two.
In quiet moments, feelings cast,
Reveal the depths of me and you.

Embrace the night, let enigmas stir,
For in the silence, we may find,
The secrets held, as thoughts transfer,
In shadows deep, our hearts aligned.

Milton Keynes UK
Ingram Content Group UK Ltd.
UKHW021000241024
450188UK00012B/513